SANKOFA
BLACK HERITAGE COLLECTION

FIRSTS

NATASHA HENRY

SERIES EDITOR • TOM HENDERSON

Ru'bĭcon
www.rubiconpublishing.com

Copyright © 2014 Rubicon Publishing Inc. Published by Rubicon Publishing Inc.
All rights reserved. No part of this publication may be reproduced, stored in a
database or retrieval system, distributed, or transmitted in any form or by any
means, electronic, mechanical, photocopying, recording, or otherwise, without
the prior written permission of Rubicon Publishing Inc.

Associate Publisher: Cheryl Turner
Project Editor: Jessica Rose
Senior Editor: Danielle Tardif
Creative Director: Jennifer Drew
Graphic Designers: Roy Casim, Sherwin Flores, Robin Forsyth, Jennifer Harvey,
Stacy Jarvis, Jason Mitchell

Every reasonable effort has been made to trace the owners of copyrighted
material and to make due acknowledgement. Any errors or omissions
drawn to our attention will be gladly rectified in future editions.

14 15 16 17 18   5 4 3 2 1

ISBN: 978-1-77058-823-3

CONTENTS

FIRSTS

Being the first to accomplish something breaks down barriers for others. Firsts can open up society's eyes and bring about change. It takes courage and dedication to lead the way; however, as Martin Luther King Jr. said, "You don't have to see the whole staircase, just take the first step."

In this book, we look at amazing Black trailblazers and all that they have achieved. You never know what you'll be the first to do! Let's celebrate our firsts and all that they have inspired.

Jarome
Iginla

Michaëlle Jean

Charles Drew

What does it take to lead the way?

NUBIA

THINK ABOUT IT

Nubia was the world's first civilization. Imagine you could go back in time and visit Nubia at the beginning. What would you want to see and experience?

Since the civilization of Nubia dates back so far, it is difficult to know the exact date it started. Researchers have suggested different dates for when Nubia began.

THE FIRST CIVILIZATION

Nubia (New-bee-ah) is recognized by many scholars as the first civilization in the world. It began along the Nile River in Africa, hundreds of years before the first communities in Egypt. Boston's Museum of Fine Arts dates Nubia back to 6000 BCE. Nubian communities were located mainly in present-day southern Egypt and northern Sudan. The Nile River was important to these communities because the surrounding area was mainly desert. The Nile provided water for people and animals to drink, fish to eat, good soil to farm, and transportation for trade and communication.

THE LAND OF GOLD

We do not know what the ancient Nubians called themselves. However, the name *Nubia* might have come from the Egyptian word *nbu* (nub), which means "gold." The Egyptians might have used this name because Nubia had a lot of gold.

BCE: *before the Common Era*

Mediterranean Sea

Egypt

Thebes

Red Sea

Nile River

Sudan

Meroe

AFRICA

Nubia at its greatest size

DAILY LIFE

The earliest Nubians were nomads. They moved to different locations in search of food. They gathered plants, hunted animals, and fished. As time went on, they began living in one location for longer periods of time. They started raising sheep, cows, and goats. They also began planting crops such as dates, wheat, and barley. They made unique pottery. They're known as some of the best potters of the ancient world.

THE FIRST MONARCHY

As their culture evolved, Nubians began staying in one area and lived in small communities that were ruled by chiefs. The chiefdoms came together as a kingdom ruled by a monarch. Nubia had the first monarchy in human history. The earliest ruler of Nubia that is known by name is King Awawa. Another powerful Nubian king was King Nedjeh (Ned-je). He is known for expanding the Nubian kingdom north, forcing the Egyptians out and taking over Egyptian forts and trading posts.

nomads: *people who move from place to place*
monarch: *king, queen, emperor, or empress who rules over a kingdom or empire*

Nubia had the first monarchy in human history. The earliest ruler of Nubia that is known by name is King Awawa.

King Piye, from the Nubian kingdom of Kush, accepting the respects of a princess

TIES WITH EGYPT

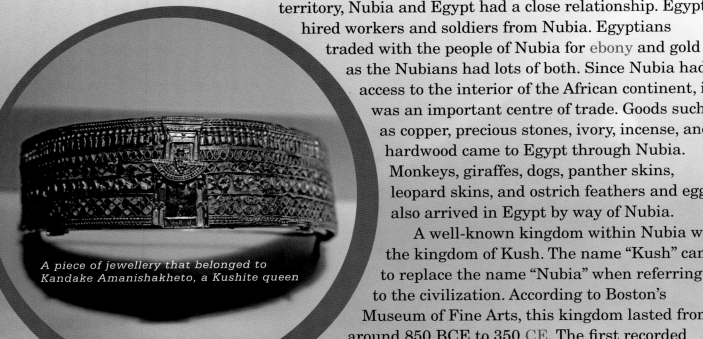

A piece of jewellery that belonged to Kandake Amanishakheto, a Kushite queen

Despite an ongoing struggle for control of the other's territory, Nubia and Egypt had a close relationship. Egypt hired workers and soldiers from Nubia. Egyptians traded with the people of Nubia for ebony and gold as the Nubians had lots of both. Since Nubia had access to the interior of the African continent, it was an important centre of trade. Goods such as copper, precious stones, ivory, incense, and hardwood came to Egypt through Nubia. Monkeys, giraffes, dogs, panther skins, leopard skins, and ostrich feathers and eggs also arrived in Egypt by way of Nubia.

A well-known kingdom within Nubia was the kingdom of Kush. The name "Kush" came to replace the name "Nubia" when referring to the civilization. According to Boston's Museum of Fine Arts, this kingdom lasted from around 850 BCE to 350 CE. The first recorded Kushite king was King Alara. During his long rule, King Alara stretched the boundaries of Kush south to the city of Meroe (Mer-oh-way).

> What do you think might make a king "legendary"?

The legendary Kushite king Piye (Py) ruled after King Alara. King Piye helped Egyptians in Thebes defend themselves against northern Egyptians. He not only saved the people of Thebes, but he also conquered the rest of Egypt. He became the first pharaoh of Egypt's 25th dynasty. Egypt remained under Kushite rule for approximately the next 100 years.

---

ebony: *wood that is blackish or dark brown*
CE: *Common Era*
pharaoh: *ruler in ancient Egypt*

Pyramids in Meroe

MEROE

According to Princeton University history professor Robert Tignor, the kingdom of Kush moved south around 300 BCE. The kingdom relocated because it feared attacks by Persian and Egyptian armies. The new royal court was built in Meroe. The city became the centre of trade for the kingdom. The artisans of Meroe made iron and bronze objects, fabrics, and beautiful gold jewellery. By the beginning of the Common Era, the people of Meroe had created a system of writing called Meroitic, which is the second oldest in Africa, after Egyptian hieroglyphic writing. They used it to record in their own language. Unfortunately, no one today has been able to figure out how to understand it.

During this era, the kingdom was ruled by a series of queens. *Kandake* (Kan-dah-kee) was the title for a queen. It means "great woman." One of the earliest known queens to rule Kush was Kandake Shanakdakhete (Shan-ak-dak-et-ee). There is a statue of her in Meroe, along with her pyramid, which is one of the biggest of the 223 pyramids built to hold the bodies of Kush rulers.

According to Boston's Museum of Fine Arts, by 350 CE, the kingdom of Kush was no more. It was conquered by the kingdom of Aksum (Ahk-soom), which is known to us today as Ethiopia.

The great civilization of Nubia influenced the other societies around it for several hundred years. Nubia was a land full of natural wealth, talented artisans, and advanced ideas. Nubia flourished in the Nile Valley and is remembered for its contributions as the world's first civilization.

Hieroglyphic writing in a temple in Nubia

< Why might other civilizations have wanted to take over Nubia?

---

artisans: *workers who usually make things by hand*
Era: *period of time*
hieroglyphic: *written using pictures*
flourished: *thrived; prospered*

CONNECT IT

Find out more about Nubia online or at the library. Imagine you lived during the time of Nubia. Write a journal entry that explores what a day in the life of a person in Nubia might be like. Share your journal entry with a partner.

The Boy and the Story

BY SHAUNTAY GRANT

THINK ABOUT IT

There are many stories about how the universe came to be. What stories have you heard?

MANY CULTURES HAVE deep roots in the tradition of storytelling. Through this oral tradition, people pass on knowledge, teach history, and share their beliefs. Stories are passed down from generation to generation.

The following is a story set in Africa. It is inspired by traditional myths and uses the author's own creative storytelling. It talks about how people first came to walk on Earth and about how the first star appeared in the sky.

ABOUT THE AUTHOR

Shauntay Grant is a writer, musician, spoken word performer, and journalist. She lives in Halifax, Nova Scotia.

What stories are shared in your family? Which of them do you most enjoy hearing, and why?

A long time ago, in a certain village, there lived a young boy who loved stories. He loved how they sounded, how the Elders' hands would dance to the rhythm of the words when they spoke. And he loved how the dust would come up when they shuffled their feet. It made him think about all the roads they must have travelled in their lives.

The Elders seemed to know secret things, all about the world and how it was born. And more than anything, the boy wanted to know their memories.

"Tell me a story," he asked an old woman one night.

The old woman was very still, but the boy could see the story bubbling up inside her.

"A long time ago," she said, "Earth was empty and dark. There was no life. The Sun, the Moon, the animals, and all the ancestors lived deep underground.

"Then one day, Earth cracked, and a giant hole appeared that went straight to the surface. The people came up from under. The world was dark, and it was new to them. They didn't know what to do. But one man had an idea."

The old woman paused, raising her right hand high above her head. "He picked up the Sun with just one hand, and he threw it far into the Sky. That's how the day was made.

"But the Sun grew tired from shining and after a while it lay down to rest, and Earth was dark again. So the man took the Moon in his hand, and he tossed it high up into the darkness. That's how the night was made."

The boy listened while the old woman spoke. He watched her decorate the story with her hands. "What about the Stars?" he asked.

"Do you see that bright Star over there?" the old woman said, pointing up.

The boy searched the Sky until he found the brightest Star. "Yes!" he shouted. "I see it!"

"Each time someone leaves Earth, all that was good in them becomes a light for the world to see," said the old woman. "That brightest light you see there, that is the soul of the man who put the Sun and Moon in the Sky. The ancestors are there all around him. But he is the first and brightest Star."

The boy's eyes grew wide with wonder. He had never heard this story before, but the old woman's words stayed with him, and they followed him to bed that night.

The next day, the boy tried hard to remember every word. But he soon discovered that it was a lot easier to listen to a story than remember all of its parts.

He went looking for the old woman.

"Where are you going?" his mother asked as he was leaving home.

"To find the old woman," said the boy. "I want to hear her story."

His mother became very quiet. She finally spoke, but only after a long time.

"My dear boy," she said. "The old woman is gone. The wind took her this morning. She's gone to be with the ancestors. She's gone to join the Stars."

The boy became sad. Now more than ever, he was determined to find the old woman's story.

"Do you know about the man who put the Sun and Moon in the Sky?" he asked his mother.

His mother smiled, and didn't say a word, but the boy could tell she knew the story—he could see it bubbling up inside her.

"Will you help me remember?" he said. "The old woman told me the story last night, but when I woke up this morning, my memories were gone."

"A story is never gone," said his mother. "What do you remember?"

The boy thought long and hard. "I remember the Sun and the Moon," he said. "And the ancestors underground."

"Is that all?" his mother asked.

The boy thought some more. "Earth cracked and made a giant hole to the top. The people came up, but they didn't understand this new world."

"Is that everything?" asked his mother.

The boy closed his eyes. He tried to remember the old woman, the way she raised her hands and threw them to the Sky. All of a sudden, he could feel the story bubbling up inside him.

"There was a man who took the Sun in his hand," he said, raising his right hand high above his head. "He had an idea, and he threw the Sun far into the clouds."

The boy was on his feet, acting out the story with his whole body.

"The Sun got tired," he said. "So the man picked up the Moon and tossed it into the Sky." The boy pulled his arm back, then threw it forward as far as he could reach.

"The man is gone now," he told his mother. "But his soul is with the ancestors."

The boy pointed to the Sky. "See there?" he said. "He is that brightest Star."

"You see?" said his mother. "Our stories never leave us, do they?"

The boy smiled. "Never," he said. And that's when he knew that the heart of the old woman's story would always be with him, now and for a very long time.

So that night, the boy sat with his family by the fire. They listened while he told them all about the Sun and the Moon and the Stars. Afterwards, he lay outside, looking at the Sky.

He thought about the old woman.

He tried to find her Star.

CONNECT IT

Research online or at the library to find another traditional story about how the Sun, the Moon, and the Stars came to be in the Sky. In a small group, take turns telling one another the story you found. Be sure to use body movements and facial expressions when sharing your story.

TRAILBLAZERS: FROM POLITICS TO POETRY

CAN YOU IMAGINE being the first person to do something important? The people on these pages knew exactly what that was like. They were trailblazers in their fields.

trailblazers: *people who were the first to do something*

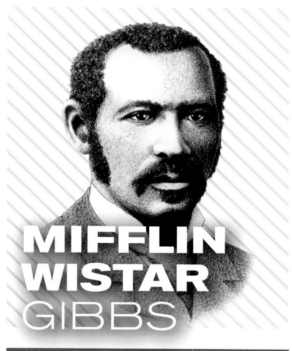

MIFFLIN WISTAR GIBBS

(1823–1915)

Mifflin Wistar Gibbs was the first Black politician in Canada. In 1866, he was elected to city council in Victoria, British Columbia. Gibbs was born in the United States. He helped enslaved Africans escape by way of the Underground Railroad in the 1840s. After living in British Columbia for 12 years, Gibbs returned to the United States.

ANDERSON RUFFIN ABBOTT

(1837–1913)

Anderson Ruffin Abbott was the first African Canadian to graduate from medical school in Canada. He graduated from the University of Toronto. He was the first Canadian-born doctor of African descent. He is best known for something that happened in 1865 near the end of the American Civil War. He was one of the doctors who took care of American president Abraham Lincoln while he was dying after being shot. Lincoln was assassinated by John Wilkes Booth.

assassinated: *murdered, usually for political reasons*

PORTIA WHITE
(1911–1968)

Portia White was a classical singer from Nova Scotia. She became a star, but the road to stardom was not easy for her. She had difficulty booking performances because of her race. However, despite this, White was known around the world for her beautiful voice. The Halifax *Chronicle Herald* called her the singer who "broke the colour barrier in Canadian classical music."

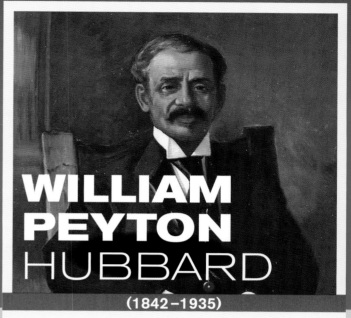

WILLIAM PEYTON HUBBARD
(1842–1935)

William Peyton Hubbard was a baker, an inventor, and Toronto's first politician of African descent. He was the child of former enslaved Africans in the United States who had escaped to Canada. He first worked as a baker in Toronto. Like most bakers, Hubbard used an oven all the time. But he thought this oven could be improved. So he invented his own. He designed a new and improved oven and got a patent for it. Then he started a company to manufacture ovens. He called it Hubbard Ovens. In addition to being an inventor, Hubbard was the deputy mayor of Toronto from 1906 to 1907.

CHARLES DREW
(1904–1950)

Charles Drew was a doctor, surgeon, and teacher. In 1933, he graduated from McGill University in Montreal with a Medical Degree (MD) and a Master of Surgery degree. During World War II, Drew led the first large-scale American Red Cross blood collection. The blood was used to treat wounded soldiers and helped to save thousands of lives.

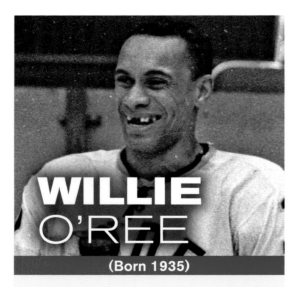

RITA DEVERELL
(Born 1945)

Rita Deverell of Houston, Texas, moved to Canada in 1967. She became the first Black Canadian woman to be a network television vice-president. She was also one of the first Black female television hosts in Canada. Deverell was one of the founders of Vision TV. This Canadian television network is the world's first multifaith and multicultural network. In the 1980s, she was the Acting Director of the School of Journalism at the University of Regina in Saskatchewan. This role made her the first woman in Canada to lead a journalism program. Among her many achievements is Deverell's place on *Maclean's* Honour Roll of Outstanding Canadians. She is also a two-time Gemini Award winner.

WILLIE O'REE
(Born 1935)

In 1958, Willie O'Ree became the first person of African descent to play in the National Hockey League. Born in Fredericton, New Brunswick, he played professional hockey for 21 years. What makes Willie O'Ree's story even more exceptional is that he couldn't see out of his right eye. He lost most of the sight in his right eye when he was hit by a puck. But none of his fans or even his coaches knew about it.

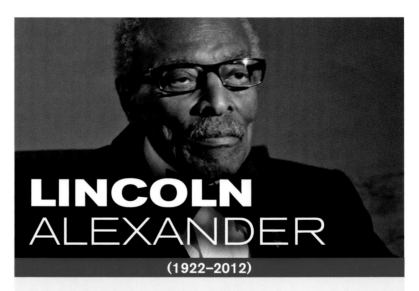

LINCOLN ALEXANDER
(1922–2012)

Toronto-born Lincoln Alexander wasn't just the first African Canadian to break one barrier. He broke many barriers. In 1968, Alexander became the first Black Member of Parliament in Canada. In 1979, he became the first Black cabinet minister in a Canadian government. Then, in 1985, Alexander became the first Black Lieutenant-Governor in Canada. When Alexander died in 2012, he was given a rare provincial state funeral. In 2013, 21 January was named Lincoln Alexander Day in Ontario.

JEAN
AUGUSTINE

(Born 1937)

Jean Augustine, who was born in Grenada, West Indies, came to Canada in 1960. In 1993, she became the first Black woman elected to the Canadian Parliament. She was also the first Black female cabinet minister in the federal government. One of her biggest accomplishments as a Member of Parliament was having February declared Black History Month. Augustine remained a Member of Parliament until 2006.

GEORGE ELLIOTT
CLARKE

(Born 1960)

In 2001, poet George Elliott Clarke of Nova Scotia was honoured with the Governor General's Award for English-language poetry. This is one of the highest honours a Canadian poet can receive. In 1998, Clarke became the first recipient of the Portia White Prize, which is awarded annually by the Nova Scotia Arts Council. Clarke has published many works of fiction and non-fiction. He has won more than a dozen awards for his work.

CONNECT IT

There are many other important "firsts" that could have been included on these pages. Use the Internet and other resources to write a short profile on Addie Aylestock, Yolande James, or another person of your choosing. Share your profile with others in your class.

EXTRA!
EXTRA!

THINK ABOUT IT

What information can you find in a newspaper? Think about why a newspaper aimed at African Canadians would have been important in the middle of the 20th century.

CARRIE BEST FOUNDED Nova Scotia's first African Canadian newspaper. She did this at a time when racism meant African Canadians did not hold a lot of positions of power. Best fought for her rights as both an African Canadian and as a woman. Find out more about this incredible woman in this timeline.

1903

Carrie Prevoe is born in New Glasgow, Nova Scotia, on 4 March. Her parents are James and Georgina Prevoe. One of Prevoe's most vivid memories of her childhood is her mother standing up to an angry mob during a race riot. This display of courage made her mother her hero and role model.

race riot: *violent fight among people of different races*

1925

Prevoe marries a railway porter named Albert T. Best. The couple has a son the next year. They also adopt two daughters.

porter: *person hired to carried baggage and other loads*

1940s

In the 1940s, African Canadians are often expected to sit in separate sections in restaurants and theatres, on buses, and in other public places.

On 29 December 1941, Best and her son, Calbert, are arrested for sitting in a section of the Roseland Theatre that is reserved for White people. They are charged, convicted, and fined for disturbing the peace.

---

convicted: *found guilty*

1952

Best begins hosting a radio program called *The Quiet Corner*. She features poetry and music. The program is popular, and Best is on the airwaves for 12 years.

1956

Best stops publishing *The Clarion*; however, she continues writing letters to the editor and articles for other publications.

1946

After years of writing poetry and letters to the editor, Best launches her own newspaper, *The Clarion*. The paper begins as a single sheet of paper.

At this time in Canada, when African Canadians are having trouble getting a seat in public places, a Black woman starting her own newspaper is a remarkable achievement. In *The Clarion*, Best reports many stories about African Canadians who are facing discrimination in public places, including hotels, restaurants, and theatres. At this time, there is no other newspaper reporting the news from the perspective of Black people in Nova Scotia.

The Clarion gives African Canadians a voice they have not had before.

---

discrimination: *unfair treatment because of race, religion, gender, or other factors*

1968

Best begins writing a column about human rights for a newspaper called *The Pictou Advocate*. Among other topics, she fearlessly speaks out against the discrimination experienced by Black property owners.

1977

Best creates a publishing company to publish her autobiography, *That Lonesome Road*.

2002

After her death, Nova Scotia gives Best its highest honour. The province awards her with the Order of Nova Scotia for her outstanding achievements.

1974

Best is made a Member of the Order of Canada. She is honoured for her lifelong work to improve the lives of Canadians.

1979

Best is promoted to an Officer of the Order of Canada. She is recognized for her exceptional achievement in serving Canada and humanity.

2001

On 24 July, Best dies in her home in New Glasgow.

1975

St. Francis Xavier University in Antigonish, Nova Scotia, gives Best an honorary degree. Seventeen years later, she is also awarded a second honorary degree from the University of King's College in Halifax, Nova Scotia.

1992

After 36 years, Best briefly brings *The Clarion* back to life.

2011

Canada Post issues a postage stamp in Best's honour. Jim Phillips of Canada Post says Best was chosen because she "fought not only for her own rights, but also for the rights of other women and minorities throughout her trailblazing career."

MARCI IEN:
MODERN-DAY REPORTER

CARRIE BEST'S STRUGGLES and successes helped pave the way for other Black women in the world of journalism. One of the women who followed in Carrie Best's footsteps is Marci Ien.

How might Marci Ien's experiences as a journalist be different from the experiences of Carrie Best?

Marci Ien was born in Toronto, Ontario. After high school, she entered Ryerson University's Radio and Television Arts program in Toronto. Even before she graduated from university, Ien was already working as a journalist. She worked as a newswriter and general assignment reporter for a television station in Hamilton, Ontario.

In 1995, Ien's award-winning news series *Journey to Freedom* got her noticed. The series was about the Underground Railroad. Three years later, Ien covered one of the biggest stories of her career — the crash of Swissair Flight 111 off Peggy's Cove in Nova Scotia.

In 2008, Ien was presented with the Harry Jerome Award for her outstanding work in journalism. The award also recognized Ien's work with children's charities, such as Children's Miracle Network. Ien has also volunteered her time with the Journalists for Human Rights program. She travelled to Sierra Leone to mentor journalists there.

In 2011, Ien landed her biggest job yet. She was named the co-host of *Canada AM*, CTV's national morning show.

When asked if she has faced any barriers because of her race, Ien said, "There are opportunities that I didn't get that I know I deserved," but she's unsure if this was due to racism. "I don't have time to focus on negativity," she says. "Life's far too short."

Ien's advice for future journalists is simple. She recommends that anyone interested in becoming a journalist try volunteering with a newspaper, or a radio or television station. She also tells aspiring journalists not to let anyone say they can't do something. "No one has the right to crush another person's dream."

CONNECT IT

What are some of your dreams for the future? Write a list of five things that you wish to accomplish in your life.

HE SHOOTS! HE SCORES!

THINK ABOUT IT

In a small group, discuss what it takes for a person to achieve his or her biggest dream.

HOW DID JAROME Iginla become one of the most successful players in the history of the National Hockey League (NHL)? Read this profile to find out.

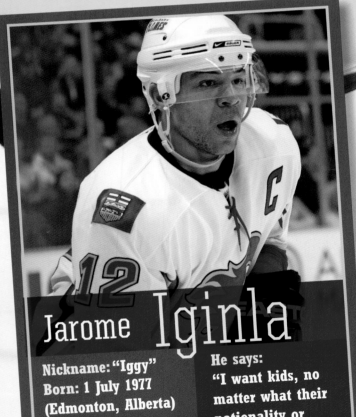

Jarome Iginla

Nickname: "Iggy"
Born: 1 July 1977 (Edmonton, Alberta)
Height: 1.85 m
Weight: 97 kg
Position: Right wing
Shoots: Right

He says:
"I want kids, no matter what their nationality or background, to dream big and think it's possible."

Before he was the hockey superstar he is today, Jarome Iginla was a boy with a big dream. He wanted to play in the NHL. But when Iginla told others about this dream, most people had the same reaction. They told him that there weren't many Black players in the league. This didn't bother Iginla. He simply reminded them of Grant Fuhr, his idol.

Grant Fuhr was an African Canadian goaltender who helped the Edmonton Oilers win five Stanley Cups in just a 10-year period.

Iginla's path to the NHL began when he was seven. That's when his grandfather introduced him to hockey. Iginla played goal, like Fuhr, for his first two years in organized hockey. Then he switched to right wing. When Iginla was nine years old, one of his biggest dreams came true. He had the chance to meet Grant Fuhr. Meeting Fuhr encouraged Iginla to work harder to make his dream come true.

Iginla played for the Kamloops Blazers before being drafted to the NHL. He was chosen by the Dallas Stars in the 1995 NHL Entry Draft and then traded to the Calgary Flames.

By the 2001–02 season, Iginla was a superstar in the NHL. He won the Maurice "Rocket" Richard Trophy as the NHL's top goal scorer. He was also the first Black player to win the Art Ross Trophy for leading the league in points. In 2002, Iginla also became the first Black man to take home a gold medal at the Winter Olympics. Just one year later, in 2003, Iginla became the NHL's first Black captain when the Calgary Flames made him captain.

By 2011, Iginla had scored 1000 points as a Calgary Flame. The following year, he scored his 500th career goal. In 2012, Iginla became only the seventh player in NHL history to score 30 goals in 11 seasons in a row. In the midst of all his success in the NHL, Iginla was also on a second Olympic hockey team that won a gold medal.

Even though he spends a lot of time on the ice, Iginla still finds time to give back to his community. It's especially important to him to meet and inspire young athletes, just as Grant Fuhr inspired him. Iginla is proud to be a role model for young people.

EVEN THOUGH HE SPENDS A LOT OF TIME ON THE ICE, IGINLA STILL FINDS TIME TO GIVE BACK TO HIS COMMUNITY.

"I have had parents of children who are minorities tell me their kids really look up to me, and that makes me proud," said Iginla in an interview.

Iginla's kindness and generosity do not go unnoticed. Former Calgary Flames general manager Craig Button had the following to say about the right winger with a heart of gold: "He's a better person than he is a player, and we all know what kind of player he is."

How might playing in the NHL be different from playing in the Olympics?

Why do you think Iginla and other athletes choose to donate their time to charities?

Iginla celebrates Team Canada's gold medal win during the 2010 Winter Olympics.

Lanny McDonald presents Iginla with a gold stick in recognition of his 500th NHL goal.

Iginla poses with the Mark Messier NHL Leadership Award following the 2009 NHL Awards.

THESE ARE JUST A FEW OF THE HIGHLIGHTS OF JAROME IGINLA'S UNFORGETTABLE CAREER.

1995: Awarded the George Parsons Trophy for being the most sportsmanlike player during the Memorial Cup

1995: Selected 11th overall in the NHL Draft

1996: Made his first NHL appearance during the Stanley Cup playoffs

2002: Won Olympic gold as a member of Team Canada

2003: Named captain of the Calgary Flames

2010: Assisted on Sidney Crosby's goal, which won Team Canada the Olympic gold medal

2011: Named to take part in the NHL All-Stars Game for the sixth time, but declined so that he could visit his sick grandmother

2013: Signed a $6 million deal to join the Boston Bruins

sportsmanlike: *fair, respectful, and polite while playing sports*

Iginla poses for a portrait in his team jersey in 1995.

Iginla skates with his children in Calgary, Alberta, for the 2011 Tim Hortons NHL Heritage Classic.

CONNECT IT

Imagine you are a sports reporter who is interviewing Jarome Iginla or another Black athlete of your choice. Write five questions you would ask him or her. First, talk with a partner about what makes a good question.

STRIKE A POSE

THINK ABOUT IT

Think about what you already know about the modelling industry. What are some reasons that it might be difficult to break into this industry?

ASPIRING MODELS DREAM of wearing a top designer's clothing, being the face of a cosmetics company, or being featured in ads on TV, online, or in magazines. But is life in the spotlight all that it's made out to be?

The North American and European modelling industries have not always welcomed people of all ethnicities into the profession. In the mid-20th century, the narrow view of beauty meant that models were almost always of European descent. Talent scouts, modelling agencies, and consumers believed that Black models did not represent the mainstream standard of beauty. This is still an issue today. Carole White, co-founder of Premier Model Management, says, "According to the magazines, Black models don't sell." Fashion photographer Steven Meisel agrees, stating that some of his clients have refused to use Black models in photo shoots. He says, "I've asked my advertising clients so many times, 'Can we use a Black girl?' They say no. Advertisers say Black models don't sell."

However, this has not stopped ambitious models. They have confronted this prejudice and opened the doors for other Black models to follow their lead and pursue careers.

Talent scouts: *people who find talented individuals to hire for a certain job*
mainstream: *regular; widely believed*
prejudice: *dislike of others that isn't fair or reasonable*

One of the models who helped break the barrier was Lana Ogilvie, a Canadian model. In 1992, she became the first Black model to exclusively promote Cover Girl cosmetics. Despite turning points such as this, Black models still face serious discrimination. To use New York Fashion Week as an example, in 2013, a mere six percent of models were of African descent. Supermodel Iman spoke to the *New York Times*. She said, "It feels to me like the times need a real hard line drawn like in the sixties, by saying if you don't use Black models, then we boycott."

Fortunately, there are magazines out there that want to see more Black models in the industry. *Essence* magazine is one of them. This publication, which was created exclusively for Black women, is filled with images of Black models. One of the models who has graced the cover of this magazine is Stacey McKenzie, an African Canadian model. There is also *UPTOWN* magazine, which was created for men and women of African descent.

In 2008, *Vogue Italia*, the Italian edition of *Vogue*, tried to address the lack of Black models in the industry. The magazine published an all-Black issue in July of that year. It became the magazine's highest-selling issue. Copies sold out in the United States and the United Kingdom in just three days. The publishers had to print an extra 60 000 copies to satisfy demand!

Although there are people fighting for more diversity in the modelling industry, this is not enough. Magazines that feature models of African descent should not be a rare find. Society needs to redefine what makes a model.

boycott: *refuse to buy, use, or participate in something in order to make a point*

> Why do you think so many people wanted a copy of this issue?

Jamaican-born Canadian model Stacey McKenzie was on the first panel of judges for Canada's Next Top Model.

CONNECT IT

Create a cover for your own fashion magazine that reflects the diversity of Canada. Pick a name for your magazine and a cover model. Add the titles of the main articles that would be found inside your magazine. When your cover is completed, share your creation in a small group.

TO THE RES

THINK ABOUT IT

Think about three superheroes you are familiar with. What qualities do these superheroes have that are the same? What qualities do they have that are different?

SUPERHEROES ARE COMIC-BOOK or movie characters who use their powers and abilities to help others. In the early days of comic-book superheroes, most characters were White. Some Black superheroes appeared in underground comic books, but it wasn't until the Civil Rights Movement in the 1960s that Black superheroes began appearing in mainstream comics. These new superheroes included Black Goliath, Misty Knight, Black Panther, Falcon, and Storm.

Each of these superheroes provides readers with a diverse cast of characters. But which of these superheroes is your favourite?

This isn't an easy question to answer. It all depends on the criterion one chooses. Is it the superhero who overcame the greatest odds? Is he or she the one who battled the most terrifying villains? Or maybe your favourite is simply the one who started fighting crime first? You be the judge!

criterion: *principle or standard on which a decision is based*

CUE!

BLACK GOLIATH

In 1966, the African American character William Foster first appeared in *The Avengers #32*. Foster worked for Tony Stark, better known as Iron Man. While working at Stark Industries, Foster created a formula that made his body grow to an enormous size. He changed his name to Black Goliath and used his size to fight crime. Even though Foster first appeared in a comic in 1966, he didn't become Black Goliath until 1975. As Black Goliath, Foster battled many evil villains, including the Stilt-Man and the Hijacker.

MISTY KNIGHT

Not only male characters fight crime. Female superheroes do their part. One of the first Black female superheroes was Misty Knight. Misty Knight made her first appearance in *Marvel Team-Up* in 1972. She was a police officer before she lost her arm in a bomb blast. Tony Stark (Iron Man) had a bionic arm made for her. It gave her superhuman strength and the ability to control machines and technology. Misty Knight is considered one of the most skilled detectives in Marvel comics.

BLACK PANTHER

The same year that William Foster first appeared in *The Avengers #32*, another Black superhero began fighting crime. Black Panther, also known as T'Challa, was introduced in *Fantastic Four #52*. Many people consider Black Panther to be the first Black superhero. Black Panther comes from a fictional nation in Africa called Wakanda, where he is king. His superpowers include superhuman fighting skills, athleticism, and intellect. He got his superpowers from a heart-shaped herb found growing in Wakanda. Black Panther eventually joined the Avengers.

athleticism: *physical skill and strength*

If you could have just one superpower, what would it be?

FALCON

Falcon is best known as Captain America's sidekick. Falcon first appeared in *Captain America #117* in 1969. He wore a suit with wings that helped him fly. He also had the ability to control birds with his mind. Falcon faced racism while growing up in Harlem, New York, but he overcame racism to become a member of the Avengers. In the 1970s, Falcon was the first Black superhero to get his own action figure.

STORM

Storm is one of the best-known Black female superheroes. She was also one of the first. She grew up on the streets after becoming an orphan at just five years old.

Unlike most other superheroes, Storm was born with her superpowers. They include the ability to control weather by creating tornadoes, hurricanes, and thunderstorms. Helped and trained by Professor Xavier, Storm became a member of the X-Men. She eventually married Black Panther, making her the queen of Wakanda. Storm first appeared in *Giant-Size X-Men #1* in 1975.

Halle Berry played Storm in the X-Men movies.

CONNECT IT

Create your own superhero or comic strip. You can make a sketch or use a website that allows you to create a superhero or a comic strip. Share your creation with your classmates and ask for their feedback.

HISTORY
in the Making

THINK ABOUT IT

What impact do you think the election of Barack Obama has had on people around the world? With a partner, discuss how his election would have affected different people.

WHEN BARACK OBAMA was elected the first Black president of the United States, he made history. His win touched people all over the world and inspired hope. Read the following newspaper clippings to see how some people reacted to his win.

CBC News, 5 November 2008

Obama a shining light for us, too: Canadian reaction

HALIFAX — Lynn Jones couldn't hide her excitement.

Jones and about 250 other Barack Obama supporters in Nova Scotia erupted into cheers early Wednesday when the senator from Illinois was declared the first Black president in the US.

Reuters, 5 November 2008

Hope washes across Africa after Obama triumph

KOGELO — Kenyans in Barack Obama's ancestral homeland danced with joy Wednesday as the election of America's first Black president sparked hope that he would tackle poverty and disease in Africa.

A young Barack Obama (top, second from left) with his grandmother and family in Kogelo, Kenya

ancestral: *belonging to a family's past*

Barack Obama is our first Black president after an inspirational race

New York Daily News, 5 November 2008

CHICAGO — President-elect Barack Obama triumphantly declared that "change has come to America."

Obama will become the nation's first African American president on 20 January.

Obama celebrates with his family after winning the United States presidential election on 4 November 2008.

THE BIG DEBATE:
Obama has taught us that "we can"

The Observer, 12 November 2008

KAMPALA — By electing Barack Obama the 44th President of the United States of America, the people of America have showed the world that hope can overcome fear and prejudice and restore the promise and allure of the American dream.

allure: *attraction; charm*

Manitobans to celebrate dawn of Obama era

Winnipeg Free Press, 16 January 2009

WINNIPEG — You can boogie to an African band. You can hang with the hipsters. You can huddle at home in front of your television or you can stay glued to your [smartphone] for live feeds from Washington.

Manitobans barely notice the low-key formality of our own prime ministerial swearing-in ceremonies, but they'll be celebrating Barack Obama's inauguration Tuesday like they elected him themselves.

inauguration: *formal ceremony to introduce someone into a position*

CONNECT IT

Imagine that you are a journalist for a newspaper. Write a headline and the first paragraph of an article about Barack Obama's win. Base your article on how his win symbolizes positive change.

33

In Her Own
WOR

THINK ABOUT IT

With a partner, share what you know about the role of the Governor General of Canada.

MICHAËLLE JEAN BECAME Canada's 27th Governor General in 2005. She was the first Canadian of African descent to hold this position. Jean was a journalist and TV host. She did this for 18 years. In 2001, she won a Gemini Award for her work.

One of Jean's goals as Governor General was to inspire young people. She was Governor General during the first half of the United Nations 2010–2011 International Year of Youth. Jean encouraged young people to work to overcome the challenges they faced. She also encouraged them to speak out and make their voices heard.

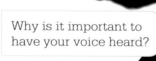

Why is it important to have your voice heard?

In these excerpts from some of her speeches, Jean shows her understanding of issues that concern young people. She encourages young people to step up to try to make a difference.

excerpts: *parts of a longer work*

D,S

> ❝ Many youth have told me that they are frustrated. **Frustrated** at being ignored. Taken for granted. And excluded when decisions are made.
>
> 'Why,' you may ask. Well in many parts of the world, we still underestimate the living force youth represent. … I have always said that you cannot build a nation by excluding youth. ❞
>
> — *Youth Dialogue on "Building for Social Change," Athens, Greece, 30 October 2009*

> ❝ Do you know the weight of your vote? Do you realize the **difference** you can make? Your voice, your ideas do count. You, the youth, are part of the solution. ❞
>
> — *Youth Dialogue on the 250th Anniversary of Democracy, Halifax, Nova Scotia, 20 September 2008*

> ❝ I know how much your concerns have to do with the **dream of a better world.**
> A world with more freedom. A world with more justice. A world that is more environmentally friendly and sustainable. A world in which wealth is shared more equitably. I say this because I have seen you in action.
>
> The world will be a better place when we fully recognize that young people are a key part of the solution. After all, you now make up more than half the world's population. ❞
>
> — *International Youth Summit MY SUMMIT 2010, Huntsville, Ontario, 25 June 2010*

sustainable: *able to last for a long time*

"**Now is the time** for you to be daring with your ideas. ... To be bold about your desire to get involved. The world is behind you, and key people are listening. Please seize this moment. The floor is yours!"

— *Youth Dialogue on the Occasion of the International Year of Youth, Ottawa, Ontario, 10 August 2010*

Jean visits a school in Dakar, Senegal.

Jean poses with young people in Budapest, Hungary.

"[The International Year of Youth] is a vision of transformation. It is a vision of **global peace** and harmony. For the International Year of Youth is about taking action. It is about dreaming big. Being bold. Pooling our resources and our ideas."

— *Youth Dialogue on the Occasion of the International Year of Youth, Toronto, Ontario, 20 September 2010*

Over the last five years of my mandate, I have travelled across Canada to **meet young people** who, with very limited resources, are addressing serious issues in their communities. Poverty. Injustice. Homelessness. Exclusion and discrimination. Environmental sustainability. Crime and violence. You name it!

— *Youth Dialogue on the Occasion of the International Year of Youth, St. John's, Newfoundland, 18 August 2010*

mandate: *period during which a government or person is in power*

CONNECT IT

With a partner, reread all the quotations. Together, choose the sentence that you both agree is the most inspiring. Compare your choice with the choice of another pair of students. Give reasons for your choice.

FIGHTING FIRES

WHILE FIGHTING INJUSTICE

THINK ABOUT IT

Have you ever volunteered? If so, how did you help out your community?

FIREFIGHTERS HAVE AN important role in society. They help protect our communities from the danger of fire. They also rescue people and respond to serious accidents. Find out how Black Canadians had to fight discrimination in order to become firefighters.

In the 1800s, African Canadians were often hired only for jobs that paid poorly and offered little chance for a promotion. They were typically hired to lay down railroad tracks or to work as waiters and cooks. Many of them wished for better jobs with better pay. Being a firefighter was such a job.

Unfortunately, African Canadians had to overcome discrimination in order to become firefighters. In 1859, members of the Black community in Victoria, British Columbia, were not welcome to volunteer for the fire brigade. In 1889, when some members of the Black community wanted to join the fire department in Hamilton, Ontario, they were turned down. White residents of Hamilton suggested a separate all-Black fire brigade; however, this never came to be.

brigade: *group of people organized to do something together*

Black workers looking for jobs as firefighters or for other government jobs often faced discrimination. Because of their race, they were kept out of jobs that served the public.

Despite this, Black men have a long history of working as volunteer firefighters in Canada. Around the late 1850s, men in Chatham, Ontario, formed the No. 3 Victoria Company. This was Chatham's all-Black fire brigade. Isaac Holden, the first African Canadian city councillor of Chatham, was the brigade's captain.

It took 65 years, but the Black community was eventually accepted into the Hamilton Fire Department. In 1954, Noel Wade and Reginald Bryant were hired as firefighters in Hamilton.

Black workers looking for jobs as firefighters or for other government jobs often faced discrimination.

In 1966, the mainly Black community of Upper Hammonds Plains, Nova Scotia, wanted to organize their own fire department. The following year, 48 African Canadian men signed up as volunteers for the Upper Hammonds Plains Volunteer Fire Department. This was the creation of the first all-Black volunteer fire department in Canada.

In 1979, Rick Bell, of Niagara Falls, Ontario, also made history. He became the first Black professional firefighter in Thorold, Ontario.

To recognize the contributions of Black men to the fire services in Halifax, the Black Cultural Centre for Nova Scotia created an exhibit in 2007. The photo exhibit was called the "Wall of Flame." It honoured 21 firefighters in Halifax.

All firefighters risk their lives fighting fires to help keep us safe. African Canadian firefighters not only fight fires, but they have fought injustice as well.

CONNECT IT

Find out how you can help make your community a better or safer place. Speak with someone at your school, a local charity, or a community centre to see how you can be of help.

LAW *and* ORDER

What do the words "law" and "order" mean to you? Discuss these words with a partner.

SINCE THE 1700s, African Canadians have been involved in maintaining law and order in Canada. Take a look at the following map to learn about the first African Canadians in law enforcement and the justice system.

Calgary, Alberta

In 1953, Violet King became the first African Canadian to graduate with a law degree in Alberta. She was also the first female lawyer of African descent in Canada.

Regina, Saskatchewan

In 1991, Julius Alexander Isaac became the first person of African descent to serve as Chief Justice of the Federal Court of Canada.

Vancouver, British Columbia

In 1972, Rosemary Brown was the first woman of African descent elected to a Canadian provincial legislature. In 1975, she became the first woman of African descent to run as a leader of a Canadian federal political party.

legislature: *group of people who make laws*

Winnipeg, Manitoba

Devon Clunis became Canada's first Black Chief of Police in 2012. He earned this position with the Winnipeg Police Service after 25 years on the force.

Ottawa, Ontario

Lori Seale-Irving was the first Black female commissioned officer of the Royal Canadian Mounted Police (RCMP). She obtained this position in 2007.

commissioned: *appointed by the House of Commons*

Montreal, Quebec

In 1999, Juanita Westmoreland-Traoré was appointed judge in the Court of Quebec. She was the first Black judge in the province.

appointed: *chosen; selected*

Charlottetown, Prince Edward Island

In 2012, Craig Gibson became Canada's first Black commanding officer in the RCMP.

Annapolis Royal, Nova Scotia

Rose Fortune, who was born in 1774, is considered by many to be Canada's first female police officer. She earned this title over the years by being a volunteer officer.

Sandwich, Ontario

In 1881, Anthony Banks became Canada's first Black police officer. He was appointed to this role in Sandwich, Ontario. Today, this town is known as Windsor, Ontario.

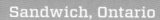

CONNECT IT

Which of the people listed on these pages interests you most? Find out more about the person at the library or on the Internet. Write a profile of the person and share it with your classmates.

STEEL DRUMS AND ICE SKATES

THINK ABOUT IT

What is something that connects you to your country? Is it a flag? A type of food? A toy? A book?

BY DIRK MCLEAN

THE FOLLOWING TEXT is an excerpt from the short story "Steel Drums and Ice Skates." It is about a young girl who leaves her home and comes to Canada for the first time. Read the story to learn about her first experiences in Canada.

ABOUT THE AUTHOR

Dirk McLean was born in Trinidad and Tobago. He moved to Canada when he was 13 years old. In addition to writing children's books, he also writes radio dramas and stage plays.

Hollie jumped up and down with joy.

"I'm going Canada! I'm going Canada!" she shouted.

Tanty Millie had just handed her a plane ticket. In the backyard of the St. James post office, Hollie hugged her Rasta doll as neighbours peeped through their windows. …

Hollie said goodbye to her relatives who lived outside Port of Spain, her schoolmates,

> Hollie speaks a form of English that is spoken by many people in Trinidad and Tobago. What do you notice about Hollie's statement?

her Brownie buddies, her favourite teacher, Mrs. Yhap Fung, and Old Tulum, the sno-cone man in front of her school.

"Hollie darlin'," he said, "I never been to Canada, but from what I hear you will have to wear five school uniforms at the same time, 'cause it *soooo* cold." Then he started to shiver, knocking his teeth together and hopping from one foot to the other. …

Back at home, Hollie helped Tanty Millie pack the biggest suitcase she owned. She wanted to make sure that she had all her possessions.

"But, Hollie, you can't take everything. There's not enough room," Tanty Millie complained.

"How will I remember Trinidad if I don't have all my books?"

"You will remember."

"But I want to take my calypso and steel band CDs and DVDs."

"Your flag I insist on, so you won't ever forget Trinidad and Tobago's colours — red, white, and black. And a Christmas cake, or your parents will never speak to me again," said Tanty Millie.

Then a sadness came over Hollie.

"I'm going to miss you, Tanty Millie. I wish I didn't have to leave you all alone."

"Eh, eh, child! You think I'm going to the cemetery or something? I'll be right here when you come back to visit."

"I know. You think I'll be able to make friends in Canada?"

---

calypso: *type of Trinidadian music*
steel band: *band that plays music on steel drums*

"Why, sure. Don't you worry yourself. Everything will be just fine," Tanty Millie reassured her.

At the airport, Hollie and Tanty Millie both cried as they embraced. Hollie thought her little heart would just burst. Then Tanty Millie watched from the waving gallery as Hollie was escorted by a flight attendant to the huge Caribbean Airlines plane.

Once in the air, Hollie was not afraid. She spent most of her time looking out of the window at the clouds and daydreaming about what Toronto must be like: gigantic skyscrapers, plenty of people, tall pine and maple trees, many toy stores, and thousands of television shows for kids. …

Hollie awoke just as the plane landed in Toronto. Looking out of the window, she saw only a blanket of white. This must be snow, that thing she'd heard so much about. She couldn't wait to touch it.

Inside Pearson International Airport, Hollie was hugged by her mom and dad. It felt safe to be held against her mother's bosom. She loved the scent of her father's spicy aftershave lotion. She wanted this moment to last forever. …

The next day, Hollie went out with her parents. When she breathed, a little cloud grew around her mouth. She stopped and looked up, noticing something strange. Very strange. The trees had no leaves. At Pape subway station, Hollie was amazed by the silver train packed with people of all shapes, sizes, and colours. Electronic advertisements announced Christmas sales at stores called Hudson's Bay, The Gap, and Indigo Books and Music. She could not believe that the train travelled underground. …

"Sweetheart, this is Sita. She lives up on the ninth floor. Sita is from India and she's going to be your new babysitter. Mom has to go to work now …" …

After Mom left, Hollie just sulked, holding her Rasta doll. She stared at this Indian stranger. Sita stared back. …

I wish Mom and Dad were home, Hollie thought.

A few days later, Sita took Hollie to city hall, where children and adults were ice-skating. A small group of little girls dressed in brown skated around the rink. Hollie stood staring. The girls sipped hot chocolate with marshmallows. They made slurping sounds and giggled.

"I used to be a Brownie back in Trinidad," Hollie told Sita.

"Really? Well, I'll take you to meet the troop near us, after the holidays."

Hollie shook her head and sat on a bench. "I don't care about being a Brownie." She stared at the dull grey sky. Once again, the sun was hiding. "I wish I was back in Trinidad," she whispered.

"Don't you like it here, Hollie?"

"No! I like walking in the snow with you and eating ice cream cones and walking through the stores in the Eaton Centre and all that. But my mom and dad work long hours *all* the time. And when Dad's home, he is sleeping and I'm all alone. Why did they send for me? I thought things would be different." …

"Well, chill! You'll get used to it. This is Canada."

"I'll never get used to it," Hollie vowed.

Early one morning after Mom took her to Pape Avenue Public School to register for classes in January, Hollie began to cry. She stamped her boots in the snow and clung to Mom's coat, refusing to let her go to work.

"Poor Hollie," said Mom. "We didn't bring you up here to be sad. But your dad and I have to work. I promise I will work fewer hours after Christmas and spend more time with you." …

That afternoon, Sita took Hollie to city hall to try to cheer her up. As they sat watching other children skate, Hollie announced, "I want to skate, Sita. Teach me?"

"Sure," Sita said, surprised. "I haven't skated even once this winter. Let's go rent some skates."

There were only a few children on the ice when Sita tied Hollie's skate laces and began teaching her to skate. But Hollie clung to her.

"It's okay, Hollie. I won't let you fall."

"I'm not afraid to fall, you know," Hollie boasted.

At that moment, they both slipped and fell. They giggled and got back up again. Hollie fell over and over. Her legs just slipped under her body like wet spaghetti. Hollie did not like this feeling at all. So they stopped and drank some hot chocolate.

Then they tried again. This time when Hollie stepped onto the ice she felt calm. She couldn't hear the traffic on Queen Street and Bay Street. The music above the rink grew faint. The icy hissing wind went still. The other skaters moved off to take a break. The sharp blades on her skates cut evenly into the ice.

Hollie let go of Sita's hand. And she glided, her long black braids flowing. Then the music came back, the icy hissing wind, the traffic sounds, the skaters. Hollie did not mind. She knew she had done something new and magical.

"You did it, Hollie, you did it!" Sita screamed. And she hugged her new friend.

Hollie and Sita skated every day for the next six days. On Christmas Eve morning, Dad came home. He brought a Christmas tree and boxes of decorations.

> Toronto is a very multicultural city. What other religious and cultural traditions are practised there?

They sang Christmas carols as they decorated the tree. Hollie loved singing "O! Little Town of Bethlehem." Next she changed the carol to "O! Little Town of Port of Spain." Then she and Dad changed the words to "O! Little Town of To-ron-to."

When they had finished, Dad lifted Hollie to place the Black angel on the top. "Can I put Rasta doll on top instead, Dad?" she giggled. They stood and looked at their creation, with the lights flashing on and off. …

On Christmas morning, she awoke in new soft yellow pyjamas with red trim. Mom had sewn her name onto the pocket. The Toronto sunlight streamed through her bedroom window, even though it had snowed all night long. For a moment, it felt like being in Trinidad. …

After slowly brushing her teeth, Hollie drifted down the hallway and entered the living room. It had been hung with Christmas decorations. Mom and Dad hugged and kissed her, wishing her a Merry Christmas and filling her world with love.

Under the flashing Christmas tree, Hollie opened her presents. The best was a pair of white leather ice skates. …

Later, Sita came by and they exchanged gifts.

"Brownie socks!" exclaimed Hollie. "I love them, Sita."

"A calypso and soca CD! Thanks, Hollie."

After Sita went home, Hollie and her parents shared some of Tanty Millie's cake and Mom's homemade ginger beer. It burned their throats, but they loved it anyway. Along with all of the Trinidadian and Canadian dishes, the sounds of Christmas carols on steel pan, and the joy and love of Mom and Dad, Hollie felt very special.

---

soca: *mix of soul and calypso music*

CONNECT IT

> In this short story, Hollie learns to skate. Think back to a time when you did something for the first time. Write a short paragraph describing how you felt.

firsts

BY SHAUNTAY GRANT

THINK ABOUT IT

In this poem, Shauntay Grant writes about people who overcame obstacles before achieving famous firsts. Why is telling their stories through poetry an effective way of celebrating these important individuals?

ABOUT THE POET

Shauntay Grant is a writer, musician, spoken word performer, and broadcast journalist. She is Halifax's third Poet Laureate (2009–2011) and this city's first African Canadian to hold this position. In 2010, she organized Canada's first national gathering of Canadian Poet Laureates. Grant has shared her blend of poetry and music internationally at festivals and events. She was also the host for CBC Radio's national Poetry Face-Off in 2008 and 2009. She has received several awards for her work, including a 2009 Atlantic Book Award for Best Atlantic-Published Book (for her children's book *Up Home*). She was given a 2011 INSPIRE Award from Big Brothers Big Sisters as well. Grant was also a Poet of Honour at the 2010 Canadian Festival of Spoken Word.

Poet Laureate: *poet who is honoured for literary achievement and who represents a certain region and promotes literature*

brave talking woman
quiet corner queen
took a thousand struggles
wrote them into dreams
advocate for freedom
a voice to call her own

bring me all your firsts
i will write them into poems

sweet, soulful singer
swaying to a tune
found her heart's desire
on a sunday afternoon
opera was her magic
'round the world she roamed

bring me all your firsts
i will sing them into poems

advocate: *person who publicly supports something*

future politician
moved from town to town
paving paths to freedom
through the underground
a voice at city council
a hero in his home

bring me all your firsts
i will speak them into poems

imaginative leader
standing on a stage
encouraging the youth
to build for social change
inspiring the masses
to make their wishes known

bring me all your firsts
i will dream them into poems

Have you ever tried to encourage others to do something positive? If so, what were you trying to inspire them to do?

CONNECT IT

Which four African Canadians is the poet referring to? Look through this book to find the answers.

Shauntay Grant

Index

Acknowledgements

Excerpt from "Steel Drums and Ice Skates" by Dirk McLean. Text © 1996 by Dirk McLean. Reprinted with permission of the author.

Grant, Shauntay. "firsts." © Shauntay Grant. Reprinted with permission of the author.

Grant, Shauntay. "The Boy and the Story." © Shauntay Grant. Reprinted with permission of the author.

Photo Sources
Cover: Michaëlle Jean–Pierre Roussel/Pierre Rousel/Newscom; **4:** black background–Attitude/Shutterstock.com; Michäelle Jean–MARK BLINCH/Reuters / Landov; Jarome Iginla–John E. Sokolowski/USA TODAY Sports; **5:** Charles Drew–Betsy Graves Reyneau, 1888-1964, Artist (NARA record: 4772241); **6:** pyramids background–Galyna Andrushko/Shutterstock.com; **7:** Kushite king Piankhy–James M. Gurney/National Geographic Image Collection/Glow Images; **8:** ring–Album / Prisma / Album / SuperStock; **9:** hieroglyphics–GYRO PHOTOGRAPHY/ amanaimagesRF/Glowimages.com; **10:** [jungle pattern–karavai; Milky Way–Roman Vanur; shapes & patterns–Viktoria; African village–Galyna Andrushko] Shutterstock.com; **11:** lady praying–Nolte Lourens/Shutterstock.com; **12:** African women–Warren Goldswain/Shutterstock.com; African boy–© Peeter Viisimaa/ iStockphoto.com; **13:** Milky Way & tree–ndphoto/Shutterstock.com; **14:** Mifflin Gibbs–creative Illustrator: Christian Elden, image courtesy of Marsha Barrow Smith; Anderson Ruffin Abbott–LAC; **15:** William Peyton Hubbard–W.A. Sherwood (1859-1919); Charles Drew–Darwinek; Portia White–Toronto Star Archives / GetStock.com; **16:** Rita Deverell–Pierre Maraval–Rita Shelton Deverell; Willie O'Ree–B Bennett/Contributor/Getty Images; Lincoln Alexander–Boris Spremo / GetStock.com; **17:** Jean Augustine–Tony Bock / GetStock.com; George Elliott Clarke–Photo by Lucas Oleniuk/Toronto Star via Getty Images; **18:** [black background–Attitude; newspaper background–d13; Nova Scotia flag–Nicku/ Shutterstock.com; **18:** newspaper clippings–© Trevor Hunt/iStockphoto.com; **19:** [mic–stockshoppe; pen ink–Jiri Hera; typewriter–Ozaiachin] Shutterstock.com; **20:** books–Stanislav Popov/Shutterstock.com; Carrie stamp–Library and Archives Canada; **21:** Marci Ien–Colin Mcconnell/GetStock.com; black background–Attitude/Shutterstock.com; newspaper clipping–© Trevor Hunt/iStockphoto.com; **22:** hockey player background–John E. Sokolowski-US PRESSWIRE; hockey player on card–Kyle Terada-USA TODAY Sports; **24:** Iginla & McDonald–Resolute; Iginla beside trophy–Photo by Bruce Bennett/Getty Images for NHL; hockey player & gold medal–ROGER L. WOLLENBERG UPI/Newscom; **25:** Iginla wearing STARS jersey–Photo by Marco Campanelli/Getty Images; Iginla & kids–Photo by Jeff Vinnick/NHLI via Getty Images; **26:** catwalk background–Dima Sidelnikov/ Shutterstock.com; **27:** Stacey McKenzie–George Pimentel / WireImage / Getty Images; **28:** halftone dots–KERVELLA rafy/Shutterstock.com; comic background–Paul Carstairs/Getstock.com; **31:** Storm–Everett Collection/CP Images; **32:** Barack Obama background–©ZUMAPRESS.com/Keystone Press; young Barack with family–ZUMAPRESS.com/KeystonePress;newspaperclip–tjhunt/iStockphoto.com; blue globe–Nicemonkey/Shutterstock.com; **33:** Barack Obama & family Photo by Joe Raedle/Getty Images; **34:** Michaëlle Jean–Pierre Roussel/Pierre Rousel/ Newscom; abstract background–Bella D/Shutterstock.com; **36:** Michäelle Jean–TAMAS KOVACS/EPA/Newscom; **37:** school kids–MOUSSA SOW/AFP/Getty Images/ Newscom; **38:** firefighter–worradirek/Shutterstock.com; **40:** [Canada map–Joe Iera/Shutterstock.com; old paper–Tischenko Irina] Shutterstock.com; Violet King–© Glenbow Museum; Devon Clunis–Steven Stotlers; Rosemary Brown–Dick Loek / GetStock.com; **41:** Lori Seale-Irving–©(2014) Her Majesty the Queen in Right of Canada as represented by the Royal Canadian Mounted Police; Rose Fortune–Nova Scotia Archives and Records Management; Craig Gibson–©(2014) Her Majesty the Queen in Right of Canada as represented by the Royal Canadian Mounted Police; **42:** [ice skates–Dmitry Veryovkin; steel drum–daseaford; snowflakes–lupulluss; grunge background–Nik Merkulov] Shutterstock.com; **44:** [Toronto vector–Emir Simsek; girl skating–chronicler] Shutterstock.com; **46:** [mic–Tarchyshnik Andrei; sky–ecco; music notes–ILYA AKINSHIN] Shutterstock.com; **47:** Shauntay Grant–Raul Rincon.